The Competent Trainer's Toolkit Series

Understanding
How People
Learn

The Competent Trainer's Toolkit Series
by David G. Reay

Understanding How People Learn is the third 'tool' in the series. The first — *Understanding the Training Function* — stands outside the training cycle. The rest, including this book, deal with the cycle stage by stage, from planning your initial strategy right through to evaluating the contribution training makes to the prosperity of your organization.

All these books can be used on training courses or as aids to self-development.

Understanding How People Learn

DAVID G REAY

Kogan Page Ltd, London
Nichols Publishing Company,
New Jersey

Published in association with OTSU LIMITED

First published in 1994

Apart from any fair dealing for the purposes of research or private study, or criticism or review, as permitted under the Copyright, Designs and Patents Act, 1988, this publication may only be reproduced, stored or transmitted, in any form or by any means, with the prior permission in writing of the publishers, or in the case of reprographic reproduction in accordance with the terms of licences issued by the Copyright Licensing Agency. Enquiries concerning reproduction outside those terms should be sent to the publishers at the undermentioned address:

Kogan Page Limited
120 Pentonville Road
London N1 9JN

© OTSU Ltd, 1994

Published in the United States of America by Nichols Publishing,
PO Box 6036, East Brunswick, New Jersey 08816

British Library Cataloguing in Publication Data

A CIP record for this book is available from the British Library.

ISBN (UK) 0 7494 1284 4
ISBN (US) 0-89397-430-7

Printed and bound in Great Britain by Biddles Ltd, Guildford and King's Lynn

Contents

Acknowledgements

This series is to a large extent based on OTSU's experiences during the past decade. Because of this, so many people have been involved in its formulation, it would be impossible to name them all. However, there are a number of people without whose help this series would not have seen the light of day.

I would like therefore to give my sincere thanks to Paul Leach for his constant support with writing, Adrian Spooner for his editing skill, Aidan Lynn for setting the series in motion, Jill Sharpe and Kathleen Gibson for design and desk-top publishing, Dorothy Reay and Amanda Froggatt for proof-reading and finally Dolores Black at Kogan Page who didn't mind flexible deadlines.

I would also like to thank Dr Peter Honey for his kind permission to refer to and include materials from *The Manual of Learning Styles* by Honey and Mumford.

Introduction

Who This Book is For

As part of *The Competent Trainer's Toolkit Series*, this book is intended primarily for trainers and professionals involved in the work of the training function. Many of the remarks I make I address to these people, and I trust that they will be able to identify with the scenarios I portray and put into action the theories I discuss.

Teachers, lecturers and students in colleges or other institutions of higher education will also find this book both interesting and useful. Traditionally, these institutions have been the guardians of most of the theories of education and learning. Be honest, if you had a question about the interaction of the mind of the learner and the subject to be learnt, you might contact the local university or college of education. You wouldn't go to the local factory, or to one of the offices in the financial district of town.

I believe the time has come for learning theory to come out of the colleges and into the factories and offices. In many places this is happening already, but the process is not complete. The trainers I have been privileged to work with in Europe and America have all expressed the view that knowing how people learn, what motivates and demotivates them, has helped to create more effective and stimulating training courses.

So, if you are a trainer looking for ways of tapping your people's undoubted potential and harnessing it into exciting, empowering, effective learning, then this book will set you well on the way. If you're a teacher, lecturer or student needing to know more of the relationship between learning theory and working practice, this book, likewise, is for you.

Objectives

By the time you have worked through this book, you should be better able to:

- describe the psychological process by which people learn
- distinguish between knowledge, skills and attitudes as targets for training
- explain the learning stages involved in the move from incompetence to competence
- differentiate between four learning styles and to administer a simple test designed to identify the learning style of an individual learner
- apply the principles and practice described in this book to training design in your organization.

Overview

To help you find your way round this book, I have prepared an overview so that you can see what is contained in each chapter.

Chapter 1 — What Learning Is

I begin with an analysis of the psychology of learning, and sift out three important descriptors of the learning process which you will be able to apply in your work situation. This leads to seven factors which your training must have if it is to match-up with and take advantage of the natural learning process.

The chapter concludes with a view of the three broad categories which cover all learning: knowledge, skills and attitudes.

Chapter 2 — The Stages of Learning

The progression from being unaware of a skill (let alone knowing how to perform any tasks needing that skill) to being able to use the skill without really thinking about it is divided into four stages. This chapter will show you how to analyse which stage your learners are at — which is vitally important, for without knowing where your learners are, you can't expect to move them on satisfactorily.

Chapter 3 — Why People Don't Learn

This chapter addresses those factors which prevent people from learning — the powerful demotivators which prevent the natural learning process from running its course.

Chapter 4 — Enabling People to Learn

Not wishing to dwell on the negative aspects of learning, Chapter 4 examines those factors which motivate people to learn, and from it you will be able to glean ideas which will allow you to harness the power of the natural learning process and turn it to the direct advantage of the individual and the organization.

Chapter 5 — Learning Styles

There are four commonly perceived learning styles, and any individual will prefer one or another of them. This chapter shows that learning is most effective when learners can apply all four learning styles to the subject matter, and that it is therefore incumbent on you to produce training which not only uses all four learning styles, but also encourages your learner to develop skills in applying all four styles.

How to Use This Book

This is not a text which you will read once and then put away never to read again (I hope!). Its inclusion in the *Competent Trainer's Toolkit Series* indicates that it is designed for you to use in your work as a trainer.

How you work through the book is really up to you. You may, if you wish, work through the pages in order from front to back and cover the whole text in that way. The book is constructed logically so that you can work right through it. Alternatively you can dip into a chapter at a time, as and when you need to.

There is a range of activities and assignments for you to complete inside each chapter. Activities are distinguished by the fact that there is some feedback — not always in the form of right or wrong answers, because there are not always hard-and-fast right or wrong answers to be had.

Assignments, on the other hand, are an opportunity for you to get out into your organization and ask some of the questions which will help you to analyse your own situation and your own needs. It would be misleading of us to include any answers although I have included comments from my own organization's experiences with a variety of clients where appropriate. However, you should bear in mind when reading these that your situation is bound to have its own unique features.

As an additional benefit, by completing activities and assignments you will be creating a body of evidence for your vocational qualification. You should keep this text and the outcomes of the activities and assignments as a record of your study.

Because the book calls on you to write your own thoughts and think about your own situation it will become your personal record and guide to your understanding of the training function.

You should feel free to write notes at any point in the margins or on the text. In fact, the more notes you write, the more useful this book will be to you in the long term.

Training and Development Lead Body Competences

A Brief Summary

Many trainers and training managers in the UK are actively seeking professional vocational qualifications, through the growing National Vocational Qualification route. This book and series can help you to achieve them. There are competences at level 3 and level 4 of the NVQ in Training and Development for which you will be able to use this book as part of your portfolio of evidence.

To make it easier for you to include the assignments in this book in your portfolio of evidence, I have prepared, on the following page, a matrix which matches a list of assignments which appear in this book and the competences which appear in the scheme booklets provided by the awarding bodies. Simply tick off the numbered assignments as you do them. Then, when you've completed this book, you can include the book itself together with any supporting documents you may create as you work through it in your NVQ portfolio. This simple matching technique will allow your NVQ assessor easily to locate your evidence and match it against the relevant criteria.

While no one assignment fulfils a whole element of competence, each assignment goes towards meeting performance criteria outlined in the elements shown. It follows that this book will make a significant contribution to your portfolio as a whole. Other books in this series will match other criteria in the TDLB list of elements.

Assignment at end of Chapter	The Assignment Counts as Evidence Towards these Elements								
1	B243	E111							
2	B211	B212	D231						
3	B243	B334	D231	E111	E112				
4	E114								
5	B311	B312							

B211   Agree a specification of requirements
B212   Identify individuals' previous learning experience and needs
B243   Adapt and agree learning programme design
B311   Identify and agree learner requirements for materials
B312   Identify and select options to meet learner requirements
D231   Modify and adapt individual learning plans
E111   Contribute to advances in training and development theory
E112   Contribute to advances in training and development practice
E114   Provide information, support and facilities to enable others to contribute to advances in training and development practice.

So Why Do You Need to Know About Learning?

The reasons why trainers should be well-informed about the way people learn have never been more pressing; and it's to East Asia that you should turn your attention if you want to focus your thoughts.

Many of the initiatives which have revolutionized business thinking and organizational attitudes over the last ten or 15 years have been shown to be effective in Japan. Total Quality, Just-in-Time, Continuous Improvement — all these have brought huge benefits to the economies of the Pacific Rim. There is also much evidence of producers in those economies who can diversify quickly into different markets, and take business away from Western organizations who have perhaps been complacent but certainly slow to react.

The notions of learning and reaction time are closely related. There is no way you can change your business overnight unless the people in that business can learn new ways overnight. And, realistically, overnight is a bit optimistic. The fact remains that the organization whose people can learn quickly has a commercial advantage over the organization whose people can't. And since no one organization has the monopoly of recruiting bright people with a track record of fast learning, it boils down to this: if the trainer knows the learning process well enough, he or she can use that ability to speed up the rate at which people can acquire new knowledge, apply new skills and adopt new attitudes.

The benefits which accrue to the organization whose people learn quickly are immediate and permanent. It is ready to react to any change of any sort, political, economic or philosophical. It can be confident that it has the resources, in terms of its people, to address any situation in the future, be it an unexpected threat from a competitor as yet unheard-of or an opportunity in a market as yet undreamt-of. And that is reassuring.

People who know they can learn become hungry to learn, and the result, in organizations where this becomes the norm, is a body of people who know about and are comfortable with all aspects of the business — from purchase and design to sales and customer care.

This of course is one of the cornerstones of Total Quality, whose advantages in terms of competitiveness are documented, so that I need not expand on that here.

On an individual level, people whose learning skills have been developed at work find themselves able to learn everything more quickly. This will of course apply in their private lives, and people will begin to notice the quality of their life improving as they find they can tackle with confidence some of the tasks they used to dread. We know of one accountant who taught herself car maintenance once she realized that she had the capacity to learn about 'that sort of thing' — and this was a direct consequence of the range and variety of training styles she met at work which developed her innate learning abilities.

Without a knowledge of how learning takes place, it will be impossible for you to design your training provision in such a way that it makes maximum use of everyone's learning ability. This harnessing of nature's gifts for the benefit of your organization and its people must be your goal; and this book will help you to achieve it.

What Learning Is

Probably because it's the way we can earn our living, we trainers tend to have a view of learning as a process that's conscious and deliberate. Something that learners choose to do and that they do in a logical and considered way.

But the reality is very different. Learning is in fact a natural phenomenon — something which all animals do to a greater or lesser extent, particularly during their maturing period, but also throughout adulthood.

By the time you have completed this chapter, you will have arrived at an accurate and justifiable definition of what learning is. You will be able to:

- list three key descriptions which place learning firmly in the field of natural phenomena
- describe seven factors which need to be present in every successful learning experience
- explain the relationship between knowledge, skills and attitude as training goals
- explain the terms **knowledge, skills** and **attitude** as they relate to training.

Learning as a Natural Phenomenon

Just for interest, you might like to ask people you know where they think they learnt the most things. Many of them, in our experience, will answer:

- at school
- at work

or mention some other structured learning environment. But in fact it is in unstructured environments that we acquire most of our knowledge, skills and attitudes.

We learn more in the first eight years of our lives than we do in all the remaining years and most of that learning is unconscious and accidental, at least from the viewpoint of the learner. Learning is extremely rapid at the beginning of our lives, and as trainers you can actually draw several important conclusions from the way a baby learns.

Think of the way a baby learns, and then look at the statements in the box below. Which statement in each pair do you think is nearer the truth? Mark it with a tick. And then, consider the implications this has for your training design.

1. Babies learn things all the time they're awake/Babies can only learn at certain times.

2. Babies and young children are naturally keen to learn things and find things out/Babies and young children don't want to learn anything unless you actively encourage them.

3. Babies and young children learn important lesson from actually doing things/Babies and young children learn by imagination and theory

If the children you know are anything like the ones I know, you'll have noticed that learning is:

- continuous
- natural
- closely related to practical experience — 'doing things'.

Each of these points is worthy of further examination now

1) Learning is a continuous process

It has been said that 'nature abhors a vacuum'. So there is never a time when we are not learning. Consciously or unconsciously we are learning new things all the time. They may be superficial — like opening the door and learning it's cold today — or profound — like learning what it means to fall in love. So as trainers, we need to recognize that learning is a natural, instinctive process.

For you as a trainer this fact leads logically to another uncomfortable reality.

The trainees who are attending one of your sessions can understand anything if it is presented in a natural way. Thus, on their way home, they may have all kinds of experiences with all kinds of consequences, and they will understand them and learn from them. For example, there is the man who drives himself home and notices a red warning light on his dashboard. If he doesn't realize it means that his battery isn't charging, he soon will — and he will have learnt it for ever.

So if there are trainees who don't seem to understand what you are saying — who knows? Maybe you have been working through a wiring diagram showing an alternator charging and a battery — then it's not because the trainees can't learn. It's your training which is not taking advantage of the natural learning process, and that's because you need to design it better.

Actually, the news is even worse. Since learning cannot stop — it **is** continuous — what those blank-faced trainees are learning is that your training is . . . well, less than ideal.

2)   We all have a thirst for learning

Have you ever watched the frustration of a child just before it
learns to read? A parent or grandparent has been reading to it.
The child **knows** that books are full of excitement, wisdom and
adventure. And yet it does not have the basic skill to extract all
that fulfilment which the book contains. Or think of the slightly
older child who keeps on asking all those difficult 'why' questions:

'Why is the sky blue?'

'Why is it raining?'

'Why do old people have grey hair?'

In both these cases, the child is desperate to learn, in order to make sense of the
universe in which it lives.

Think too, of all informal learning projects in which we get involved. Stop for a
moment and consider your friends, relations or colleagues at work who have decided
to learn something new. A foreign language perhaps, or car maintenance, or oil
painting. People are prepared to invest a lot of time, money and effort to learn the
things which interest them.

But some of your training provision probably doesn't affect people like that. Instead
of switching them on to learning — which is the natural state of affairs— it switches
them off.

What has happened to stall the natural thirst for learning?
And how can you overcome this difficulty?

Write your answers to those questions here:

.

.

- The benefits of learning have either:
  — not been made clear
  or
  — been concealed
- The solution is to make the benefits clear at all times.

If we can channel this thirst for skills and knowledge towards relevant objectives, we will be amazed at the enthusiasm people will show.

If you are involved in training which has no benefit to the people, then you are onto a loser, and you should consider changing the content of your training provision as soon as possible. This situation is rare, however.

The reality of the situation is that there is a continuum. The greater the perceived benefit, the greater will be the thrust to learn, and so it may well be worth your while examining ways of selling the benefits of your training.

3) Learning comes from doing

You may well have been amused to watch a young child trying to force a large toy into a small box. It will become increasingly frustrated, then give up in disgust. A minor incident like that is really a major event. In educational jargon, the child is learning spatial relationships — the size comparison between different objects.

From your point of view as a trainer, you should notice the strength of 'doing' as a means of learning. This is nature at work, and you can harness it, but you can't resist it. Thus if your trainees learn one way of working in theory and then return to the workplace where the reality of their situation forces a slightly different way of working on them, then it is the 'real' situation which will be learnt. It will override any theoretical learning which may have happened earlier. Learning through theory is an acquired skill, and learning through doing is a natural skill.

The key elements in learning through doing are the consequences of success and failure. Do something right, and you get a reward — be it mere satisfaction, food, money or other reward. Do something wrong and you suffer — be it frustration or pain; and your natural drives towards reward and away from suffering encourage learning.

This has one major implication for you as a trainer — it determines what it is that you do all the time in your job.

What is it that you do (or should do) all the time in your job? And here's a clue: you are *not* there to *teach*.

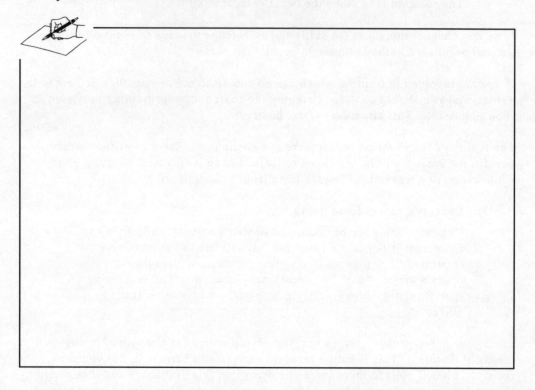

You are not there to teach, but to help people to learn. Your function is that of facilitator, creating opportunities for learning by setting up experiences from which people can learn for themselves.

You can usefully extend these conclusions from the natural learning process to draw up some key factors of learning psychology.

We are going to present those key factors — there are seven in total over the next few pages. Please don't infer that there is some hierarchy simply because we are presenting the factors one after another. There is no hierarchy. Learning must contain all these factors or it will fail. You may find it useful to judge your training against these factors to see if you can find any weaknesses in it, or to confirm its soundness.

1) **Motivation, or a sense of purpose**

People learn when they can see a worthwhile end-product to the process. Unless you, as trainers, can provide a convincing answer to the trainee's question 'What's in it for me?' you cannot expect your training to be effective.

Case Study

A major insurance company ran very popular residential courses for its middle management in hotels across the country, but when a new trainer took over the courses, she found that many of those attending had covered much of the subject matter at previous residential courses. She described the structured learning sessions as 'a bit of a yawn' because many people were so familiar with the concepts.

And yet, the courses were popular — so what was 'in it' for the people which made them so popular?

Why were these residential courses popular?

They were popular because:
— they allowed people from different offices to meet and swap ideas
— they were a change from the routine.

The trainer restructured the courses so that trainees still got the chance to meet and benefit from a change of routine, but also met new ideas in the learning sessions — ideas which they were convinced they needed to know about. Indeed some of the sessions were organized so that the ideas which were spawned when people met became the subject matter of the course, and were discussed in a structured way. The result was a huge increase in the cost-effectiveness of the training sessions.

The existing course material was, incidentally, made into open learning materials so that new staff or those in need of a refresher could look at it when they needed it.

2) Relevance to personal interest and choice

We should not assume that statements like 'The company will benefit' or 'You've got to, it's in your job description' will necessarily turn people on. In fact, being frank, it will probably turn people off. Learning psychology is more complex than that and requires you to identify the individual motivation of trainees. There are ways of tapping into people's personal interests and choices, but they are too numerous to explore here. You'll look at the subjects of motivation and personal interest in Chapter 3 of this book.

3) Clear goals or objectives

Only if you are very lucky or charismatic will your trainees take what you ask them to learn on trust. Somehow or other the trainees have to decide for themselves whether or not it is worth their while to study what you are suggesting. The overbearing, bossy approach — 'Learn this because I say so' — won't work. Some people will resist, and rebel against learning. Others will be intimidated into cooperation, but won't learn effectively. It is more effective to set clear goals or objectives for learning, to enable trainees to decide whether it's worth putting effort into the learning process.

4) Practice and learning by doing or trying

Trainees who are committed to the learning objectives you have
offered them will be keen to get stuck in — they won't want to
debate the theory when they could be having a go themselves.
Moreover, as we've seen from the example of childhood learning,
people learn most effectively by doing.

There is an old saying:

'I hear and forget. I see and remember. I do and understand.'

Understanding is central to effective performance and only doing
can really promote understanding.

For proof of this you could consider a game you have learnt how to play. While
field games are good examples, board games are better. The theory of how to play
appears on the inside of the box lid, but by the time you are down to rule 21 out of
60 you feel the urge to make a start on the game itself and see what happens. And
later, when you have played the game a couple of times, you really understand how
to play. If you had only read the rules twice — would you have really understood?

5) Freedom to make mistakes in safety

Of course, learning by doing also means that people run the risk of
failure. However, failure in a training environment is far less
painful to the individual, and most of all to the organization, than
failure in the real world. So a key factor of learning psychology is
ensuring that people know that it is safe and permitted to fail. In
certain industries there is a long and successful track-record of
training which allows mistakes in a safe environment. Airlines
train their pilots in simulators — a lot less risky than landing a real
Jumbo in a real blizzard. This example is of course very
sophisticated, and many trainers have neither the resources nor the
need to go to such lengths. But all trainers need to create a
supportive environment in which trainees can either learn from
their mistakes in private or feel confident that their fellows are in
the same situation and will support them through it. We'll develop
these ideas later in this book.

6) **Self-checking on progress**

Learning by doing, or learning from your mistakes, implies the need to gain timely feedback on performance. You'll recall that the child learns spatial relationships because a big toy won't fit in a small box — that's instant feedback! The do-it-yourself enthusiast whose ceiling light falls to the floor after 12 months gets feedback, but a little too late for him to see exactly what he did wrong so that he will know how to correct it next time. So, as trainers, we need to remember that trainees learning a technical skill, or a complex procedure, need some inbuilt method to tell them if they're doing it right. So you need to assess the relative costs of providing immediate, practical feedback — a trainer on hand to comment on his observation or some kind of simulation may suffice, or perhaps a line manager or an experienced colleague who would coach the trainee through actual performance, at the workplace, of the skill or procedure being learnt. There would have to be some way of identifying the mistakes before they got out and did any real damage.

7) **Freedom for the trainee to learn in his or her own time, at his or her own pace**

Text-based open learning often boasts its ability to match the learner's need to learn at their own speed, in their own place. But all learning must address the learner's perspective, or it will fail. Thus we recommend that if you run courses, you allow the trainees to decide if and when they are ready for that course, and give whatever support they may need to enable them to make the right decision. Similarly with examination-based courses, we recommend that people only prepare for and take examinations when they are ready.

Knowledge, Skills and Attitudes

So far in this book we've been talking about learning as a process, and so it is. Now, however, it is time to examine what this 'learning' is which gets into your head. People say 'His head's full of learning' — but what does this learning consist of?

Well, we believe that all learning breaks down into knowledge, skill and attitudes. The child squeezing the large toy into the small box learnt:

> Knowledge: Large into small won't go
>
> Skill: How to manipulate a toy and a box at the same time
>
> Attitude: This is frustrating!

So now, over to you to see if you can identify knowledge, skills and attitudes in a piece of learning.

All learning can be broken down into these basic areas. Let's look at a simple example to make sure you're comfortable with the idea.

What's involved in wiring a plug?
Think of the task of putting a plug on the end of a piece of flex.
What knowledge, skills, and attitudes are required to carry it out properly?

Knowledge _____

_____

Skills _____

_____

Attitudes _____

_____

Here are our thoughts on the matter. When wiring a plug you need the following:

Knowledge: Which colour wire to attach to which terminal
Purpose of the fuse and fuse loads
General principles of electrical appliances

Skills: Using a screwdriver and fitting a screw
Matching plug halves
Cutting and stripping wire

Attitudes: Importance of making the appliance work
Need for safety.

As a trainer you will have a strong realistic streak in you, and you will be wondering whether the learning involved in some of your organization's more complex operations doesn't in fact break down into yet more complex areas, and the answer is, no. Any task, no matter how complex, breaks down into the three areas of knowledge, skills and attitudes.

You might find it helpful now to consider a task that's relevant to your organization.

Specify a task _____

_____

Knowledge required: _____

_____

Skills required: _____

_____

Attitudes required: _____

_____

We can now put some description to these areas of learning:

> **Knowledge:** is sometimes called 'cognitive' learning. It covers any learning to do with facts, procedures or concepts.

> **Skills:** are sometimes referred to as 'motor' or 'psycho-motor' learning. It means learning about physically **doing** something.

> **Attitudes:** are sometimes known as 'affective' learning and are to do with the way we **feel** about tasks.

The importance of categorizing learning into these three areas is that each category can be learnt most effectively in different ways.

In the box below, opposite each of the areas, write down a training method which you believe would allow learning in that area to take place.

Knowledge:

Skills:

Attitudes:

- **Knowledge:** can be gained from manuals, open learning or computer-based training. There is no need to practise anything in order to know about it.

- **Skills:** on the other hand, usually require a three-stage approach
  — tell the trainee how to perform the task
  — show them how
  — let them do it, but offer coaching support

  It is best if this takes place in a practical setting — if not 'on-the-job' then in a really accurately simulated environment.

- **Attitudes:** are probably the most difficult to change and are best tackled by a combination of discussion and experiential learning. Good open learning allows this to happen as the learner uses the activities in the text to contribute to his or her own perceptions and attitudes and then finds them confirmed or changed by what happens next. Staff supporting open learning also get a chance to discuss the trainee's feelings with them.

This does not paint the whole picture, of course. There are people who gain a lot of knowledge about, say, a machine after months of operating it, but without particular reference to a manual. Experienced computer operators 'know' when the document they are working with is being pushed to the limit. Experience tells them that the document may become difficult to open, and information may be lost. None the less the above statements are a useful guide.

Summary

In this first chapter you have seen a brief but important examination of what learning is.

First, you saw that:

- learning is a continuous process. We can't stop learning, even if we try, and your trainees are always learning something
- wanting to learn is a natural state of affairs. Knowing how to do something is associated with success; **not** knowing is associated with failure
- learning comes from doing. Only when you can **do** something can you actually claim to understand how it is done.

There are implications for you as a trainer. The more you can harness these natural learning phenomena, the more successful your training will be. To assist you in your endeavours, we described, in turn, seven key factors in learning psychology. All successful learning:

- encourages motivation and has a sense of purpose
- is relevant to personal interest and choice
- has clear goals or objectives
- involves practice, or learning by doing or trying
- gives trainees freedom to make mistakes in safety
- involves self-checking by providing timely feedback
- allows the trainees to learn in their own time, at their own pace.

Finally, you saw how the learning which enters people's minds is divided into knowledge, skills and attitudes, and that different training methods are needed for each of those areas.

Assignment:
Examine one element of your training provision, and assess it against the following criteria:

- *Does it have a sense of purpose?*
- *Is it relevant to learner choice?*
- *Has it clear goals and objectives?*
- *Does it involve practice?*
- *Are trainees free to make mistakes in safety?*
- *Does it provide feedback?*
- *Can learners learn at a slower or faster rate?*

If the answer in every case is yes, then well done. That element appears to be in tune with good learning theory. You should move on and examine all your elements likewise.

If there are some 'nos' or even 'not sures' then you will need to change something about your training — even if it is just making clear the aims and objectives of a particular item, or involving some on-the-job coaching. A matrix like the one below may well help you:

Item	Criteria not met	Corrective action	Date

The Stages of Learning

Learning is rarely, if ever, instantaneous. It is arguable that doing something dangerous and hurting yourself teaches you never to do it again; for example you may have tried to take a hot plate out of an oven without a glove or a cloth once, but not twice. But this negative kind of learning which allows you to know what not to do is not the same as positive learning which can show you what you ought to do. The negative can act as a spur to you. So if you know a plate is hot then you know not to touch it, and then you need to learn ways of handling it safely — but it cannot count as a whole learning point in itself.

Since learning is not instantaneous, then it must be a process or a progression. By the time you have finished this chapter you will be able to:

- describe four stages of the learning process
- explain how you can use your knowledge of the four stages to increase the effectiveness of your training provision.

Stage 1 — Unconscious Incompetence

Taking a truly global view, there are many skills which we are completely unaware of — in remote cultures, in obscure professions. But this complete unawareness is not 'unconscious incompetence'. There are plenty of skills closer at hand in which we are unconsciously incompetent. There are tasks which people perform so naturally that it's only when you stop to think about them that you realize there must be learnable skills involved. It's at this stage — stopping and thinking — that you realize that up till now you have been unconsciously incompetent.

The most often quoted example of unconscious incompetence is that of small children in a car. They can't drive it, but they don't know they can't drive it. A more business-orientated example would be junior office staff who could not manage the office, and aren't aware of the fact. Office management 'just happens' for them.

Before training starts, trainees may be conscious that they are about to learn something, but unaware of the complexity and detail of their learning goals. To begin to want to learn, the trainee has to move on to the next stage.

Stage 2 — Conscious Incompetence

At this stage in the popular learning-to-drive example, the driving instructor has pointed out to the learner the need to master clutch, brake and accelerator, to learn how to manoeuvre the car, to practise reversing and so on.

We'd like you now to put yourself in the learner's position — not necessarily the learner driver's, but any learner's — and think hard about this question. What is it that you now need as a learner?

We believe there are a number of things the learner needs, and so we have left you a sizeable box to write in at least four or five key needs. There is also space for you to say why you feel these needs are important.

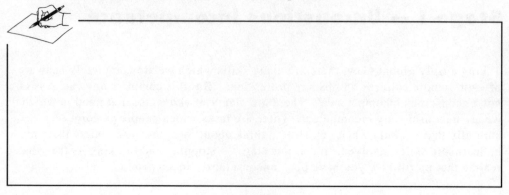

Here is our list of needs:

- **The need to change.** Learning is all about adopting new behaviours and attitudes, and that in turn means abandoning old behaviours and attitudes which is — or can be — an unsettling experience. This leads you to the next need.

- **The need for encouragement.** Being aware of how much you have to learn can be daunting. It appears to many to be a mountain to climb. Encouraging words like, 'Everyone feels like that to start with' can work wonders.

- **The need for aims and objectives.** The 'mountain' to be climbed is tackled in the same way as any other: one step at a time. You, the trainer, need to map out the steps in sequence.

- **The need to see the benefit.** You have to be able to explain 'what is in it' for the learner, or there won't be enough motivation there to allow effective learning to take place.

- **The need to own the situation**. The learner must feel fully involved in the training. They must feel that they are doing the learning for their benefit, that they have to address their own problems and challenges. They must feel responsible for their own progress. The alternative scenario is one where learners perceive that training is imposed on them. In this case, there is little commitment, enthusiasm or involvement.

If these needs are not met, then the learning will stop. People will realize they are incompetent in a certain skill and will react in a number of ways:

1) Frustration: 'I know I could manage that if I got a fair crack of the whip. . .'.

2) Wishing: 'I wish I knew more about . . . — then I'd be all right'.

3) Alienation: 'I could do that job if I wanted to but I don't want to'.

If these attitudes are prevalent in your organization then it is a sign that your training provision could do more to meet your learners' needs at the 'conscious incompetence' stage of learning.

If, however, you do meet your learners' needs, they will progress to the next stage.

Stage 3 — Conscious Competence

You may well remember passing your driving test at this stage! You were still aware of the techniques, physical actions and routines involved in driving itself. And (if you pass the test) you feel the relief of meeting a generally accepted standard.

Conscious competence, therefore, does not mean that you can perform a task and you know that you can perform it. Rather it means that you can perform a task but you are still at the stage where you have to make a conscious effort if you are to achieve the required standard.

We could summarize this stage by saying that conscious competence combines an awareness of new-found ability with an awareness of meeting a standard or objective. It's as well to remember that this is generally the stage at which the trainer's involvement finishes. At the end of training, we've got our trainees to the point where they can do the job to the required standard, but they are still having to think and concentrate very hard. From this it becomes clear that the end of training does not signal the end of the learning process.

Stage 4 — Unconscious Competence

This is the final stage of learning, when at last we don't have to consciously review the core parts of our learning each time we do something. It's become second nature, part of our inbuilt toolkit of skills and abilities.

As trainers, we only get the chance to see this stage when we go out to the workplace to see our own former trainees actually doing the job. But to acquire this unconscious competence, they still need regular supervision, support and advice. To be effective as trainers, therefore, you must ensure that line managers are competent to follow-up the training you have provided. This could mean inviting line managers into your training sessions if they take place away from the usual area, or encouraging line managers to observe training you organize 'on the job'. Ideally you will be able to delegate some initial training responsibilities to line managers so that the learners can relate to their immediate bosses throughout **all four** stages of the learning process.

You must also look carefully to your training provision if stage four of the learning process is to be successful. What particular qualities must your training provision have to allow 'unconscious competence' to follow naturally from what you have taught?

Write two qualities in here.

The training must be **practical** and **relevant**.

If it isn't you'll find line managers deliberately introducing alternative methods and short-cuts in order to meet deadlines or cost parameters. This is just another example of the need for training to be rooted in the real world.

Summary

In this chapter you have seen that there are four stages of learning:

1) Unconscious incompetence

2) Conscious incompetence

3) Conscious competence

4) Unconscious competence

You saw that these stages have great significance for your training provision, for the learner has different needs at different stages, and if your training fails to meet those needs, then correct and appropriate learning cannot take place.

Assignment:

Select four or five people from different levels of the hierarchy in your organization and find out how they feel about somebody else's job. If there is a clearly defined career structure, finding which job to quiz them on will not be difficult — it will simply involve your finding out what is the next step in the career structure.

The key questions to ask are:

- *What do you think the job involves?*
- *What training do you think you would need to do the job adequately, if any?*
- *Do you feel you could ever do that job?*

From the answers, you'll be able to tell which stage of the learning process the people are in. This will in turn allow you to diagnose their need and design your training provision accordingly.

Be particularly vigilant for signs of disaffection or frustration; these are symptoms of training which is, at present, failing to meet needs.

Why People Don't Learn

The first two chapters have stressed just how natural the learning process is. It's human nature to learn all the time — you can't help learning. So why this chapter on **not** learning?

Put simply, the fact is that people don't always learn what they are supposed to learn, or as effectively as they could — and trainers faced with these all too common situations have been known to react by wringing their hands and asking, 'Why aren't they learning?'. Of course, we know that they **are** learning, and that the real problem must therefore be that something is preventing them from learning the right things.

By the time you have finished this chapter, you will be able to:

- · identify six areas in which obstacles to learning occur
- · spot the symptoms within each area which indicate that learning is being disrupted
- · recognize the implications of these obstacles for your training provision.

So that you don't think we're being too negative, we must stress that Chapter 4 looks in detail at factors which positively encourage people to learn, so that on finishing both this and the next chapter you will be able to find ways of eliminating the negative and emphasizing the positive at the same time. Our decision to begin with the negative aspects comes from our experience that many trainers inherit situations where there are serious blocks to learning to reckon with. They feel, and we agree, that this situation is serious enough to warrant our immediate attention.

Think of some training you have had on a particular topic — or a subject at school or college, if that's more appropriate — which you just couldn't learn. Why was that, in your opinion? Write your answer in here.

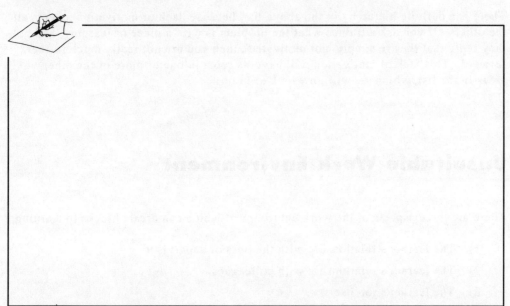

We are unable to guess your specific answer, but it is likely that it lines up with one or more of the common blocks to learning which we have listed here:

- Lack of motivation
- Unsuitable work environment
- Inappropriate subject matter
- Past experience
- Self image
- Inadequate study skills
- Poor memory

Lack of Motivation

There is a definite hierarchy in the above list, because 'lack of motivation' covers all the others. If you ask a trainee what the problem is with a piece of learning, and they reply that they're simply 'not motivated', then you are not really much further forward. This lack of motivation will have its roots in one or more of the other areas in the list, which we will now look at in turn.

Unsuitable Work Environment

There are three aspects of the work environment which can create blocks to learning:

1) The learner's relationship with the boss or supervisor

2) The learner's relationship with colleagues

3) The learner's job itself.

In the box below, write down how you feel each of the above could sour the learning experience.

1) **Relationship with boss** _____

_____

2) **Relationships with colleagues** _____

_____

3) **The learner's job** _____

_____

1) With the **boss or supervisor**. The boss's attitude to the learner or learners is as important as theirs to him or her. Does the worker feel valued? If not, they may feel that the training is some sort of slur on their competence and capacity to do the job. Do they feel important to the company, or mere appendages? If they do feel like appendages, then they cannot perceive that the training they are receiving is an investment in them. Consequently the training which you are providing in the belief that it is an investment rather than a cost will, ironically, be interpreted as exactly the opposite by the people who are supposed to benefit from it most.

The implications are that you must, as a trainer, ensure that line managers support your training provision. Support means commitment to its philosophy as well as its specific aims and objectives so that everyone understands what training is for, why it takes the form it does, and what their contribution is. If you can communicate this successfully, then managers will be able to encourage learning, and not hamper it.

2) Relationships with **colleagues or workmates** are important too.

   - What are they doing?
   - Have they had more or less training?

   Although poor working relationships are damaging in themselves, good ones can also create problems. For example, one selected from a group for special training may suffer from resentment — or feel rejected by mere harmless banter. If that happens, training in turn might be resented by the learner!

So as a trainer, you have a responsibility to create an environment suitable for learning within the organization.

3) The learner's **work or job** is equally important as a potential barrier to learning.

- Is it the right job for the wrong person? We all know people who have really thrived in one job and then moved into another which simply didn't suit them.

- Is the job challenging, exciting, or at least valued? If so, well-designed training can prepare any suitable candidate to meet its challenges.

- Or is it dreary, without status and unrecognized? The trainer may have no responsibility for job design, but if we do not, we should not expect training to put fulfilment into an unfulfilling job.

Inappropriate Subject Matter

The best planned learning experience can fail just because it is — or seems to be — irrelevant to the learner or the job.

Case Study

Mandy Wainwright left school aged 17 with good qualifications and then moved onto a hairdressing course at the local college. After a successful spell in an independent salon she moved into a large organization with a proper career structure. She was quickly promoted to the position of assistant salon manager — as is often the case in industries with a high staff turnover — and became eligible for the management training course.

This course had proven success over the previous four years and had been enthusiastically received by everyone who went on it, save those who had no aptitude for the arithmetical side of things — targets, percentages, taxes and the like — most of whom had declined the post of assistant manager anyway. Mandy was a capable mathematician, good with people, respected by her colleagues, articulate . . . yet despite having all the attributes of a good manager, she learnt very poorly on the course.

The reason was that Mandy wanted to pursue another track — an artistic one — to become a designer and technical expert rather than a manager. The course was, in Mandy's case irrelevant — or even worse: a distraction from where she wanted to go.

If training materials are irrelevant to the job, or contradict it, as in the case of machines or equipment which differ in reality from the training manual — what are the inevitable consequences?

Write your answer in here.

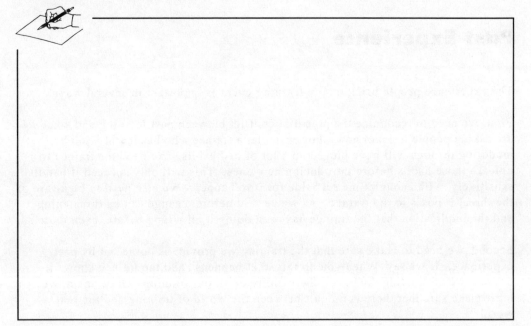

- The training function loses credibility
- That particular piece of training falls (rightly) into disuse
- Future training packages are regarded with great suspicion.

The same thing happens if the procedures or programmes you train people in don't reflect the best examples of current accepted practice. It's the **training** which is questioned. Training must be both relevant and accurate, or it will fail.

Past Experience

The experience people bring to any learning event is important in several ways.

First, we need to recognize the potential conflict between past learning and what we are asking people to learn now. For example, a trainee who has learnt a job by muddling through will have picked up a lot of bad habits. We need the trainee to unlearn those habits before introducing new ones. This will only succeed if handled sensitively, with enough time set aside for it to happen. We also need to be aware of the threat it poses to the trainee. As we've said before, change can be threatening and the implication that the trainee has been doing it all wrong before, even more so.

Second, we need to make sure that the training we provide is borne out by past experience. If we say 'When you do this, that happens', and the trainee knows it doesn't, we are casting doubts on the validity of all our training. Once again, we must make sure that there is no gulf between the world of training and the real world.

Finally, if we are asking trainees to change past habits, we must give them convincing reasons for it. 'Doing it that way could lead to the following accidents' is more convincing than 'Do it this way because I said so'.

Self-Image

This is not the place to launch off into a psychiatric discourse on the nature of the individual or the deeper recesses of the mind. From the trainer's perspective, the learner's self-image comprises two elements:

· the sum of their experiences
· self-esteem.

You could use yourself as a guinea-pig. If you are asked to talk about yourself, before long you will be mentioning things you like and don't like, the way you react to different situations and types of person. This is all material you have learnt through experience. You will probably also mention your job — the bits of it you feel comfortable with and enjoy, the bits of it which worry you; this is closely linked to self-esteem — your idea of what you are capable of.

You need to be aware that training can threaten both aspects of self-image. It can undermine past experiences and diminish self-esteem.

Can you think of one situation — very common in industry today — where trainees feel their past experiences to be definitely under threat? And what implication does this have for your training? Write your answers in here.

Situation where past experiences are threatened:

_____

_____

Implication:

_____

_____

The classic situation is where there is retraining for people whose old job is no longer required, because it implies that the job had no value. The implication of this situation is that you need, as far as you can, to build on the old skills, not discard them.

Second, any training that itself threatens self-esteem is an obvious learning block. Fear of failure is a powerful turn-off, so we'd like to ask you to think again of the need to create a positive, supportive learning environment. This is much preferable to allowing the trainees to face the risk of ridicule. Unless the trainer can both understand and reduce the threat to each learner's self-image, they won't even begin to learn.

Inadequate Study Skills

The block to learning here is lack of study skills, or lack of skills appropriate to a particular learning experience.

You should think first about what study skills actually comprise. For many people who have come through schools and colleges, study skills will be mainly comprised of:

- reading in depth
- reading for information at speed
- answering questions
- note-taking
- summarizing
- examination routine
- time planning — allowing time to study, learn and revise in a busy life.

Graduates may additionally be versed in:

- research skills
- questioning skills.

For other, non-academic types, study skills may be comprised of:

- observation
- imitation
- use of check-lists.

Each of the items mentioned previously could merit a chapter in itself, but to you as a trainer only the following point is key: if your training requires the learner to use study skills which they haven't got, then you have two choices:

- either give the learner the study skills — which we recommend, because it empowers people to learn more and more

  or

- change the style of your training so that it corresponds with the learner's existing skills.

To fail to adopt either of these is to reduce the effectiveness of your learning. De-motivation is the inevitable result.

You need now to think about who **lacks** study skills.

Think for a moment about some of the people you may be training. Which of them lacks the most study skills? Don't write names, just a description of age, background and the like will do. Put your answer in the box.

The person/persons most lacking in study skills:

-

You may well have included a young person who left school with few or no formal qualifications.

You might be surprised at the idea that a graduate could be in the same position! Yet, however able people were to pass exams in formal schooling, the study skills they had then could be very rusty today. Ask around and you may hear comments like these:

> 'It's years since I read anything other than the local paper'
>
> 'Will I have to do much writing? I don't use a pen much nowadays'
>
> 'It's all very well saying "study this and note the main ideas" but I wouldn't know how to begin!'

So when you are designing training, you have to take learners' **present** study skills into account. But does good training simply leave people with study skills that are no better than when they began?

We think not. Any learning should enable the learner to become better at learning itself. In a world where jobs and skills change so quickly we all need to improve our learning skills. So to summarize, the demands of any learning experience must:

- be carefully designed within the learner's study capability
- also enable the learner to become better at learning in the future.

Memory

We've probably all met the situation where a trainee has remembered with total clarity a few bits of a training session, but forgotten all the rest — often resulting in some major misunderstanding. This leads in turn to trainees becoming suspicious of training — and with some justification. You see, this trick of the memory is a reflection, not on the trainee, but on us as trainers.

In any short learning activity, what exactly is it that trainees will tend to remember? Write your thoughts in the box.

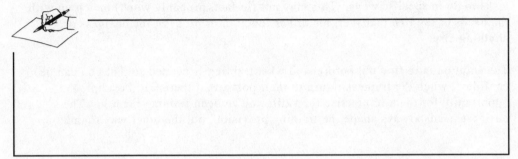

Trainees remember:

- the first thing learned
- the last thing learned
- anything that seemed vivid or exciting
- anything that was repeated in interesting ways and so held their attention.

These points have important implications for the structure and design of any learning activity. There is the need for:

- easy, step-by-step chunks
- lots of practice
- obviously attainable goals.

We can add to this list several factors that cause people to forget:

Time Between Learning and Doing

A training experience may have led to some very positive changes to knowledge or behaviour. If these are not used or practised on return to work, they will quickly be forgotten. Part of the trainer's role is to ensure that our trainees get regular practical reinforcement once they have completed their training. This does not mean, of course, that you can go to line managers and insist that trainees be given specific tasks to do in specific ways. This may not (in fact, probably won't) match up with the needs of the line manager, his or her function or process, the business or anything else.

The solution is to find out beforehand what training is needed so that you can be confident, when the trainees return to their posts, that there will be ample opportunity for them to practise the skills you've been training them in. The business needs always shape the training provision, not the other way round.

Tiredness and Loss of Concentration

The optimum attention span is just 10 minutes. After 20 minutes people tend to flag. What are the implications for your training provision of this proven and observable fact? You can't train people for 20 minutes at a time and then let them return to their duties, so what are you going to do?

Write down some tactics in this box.

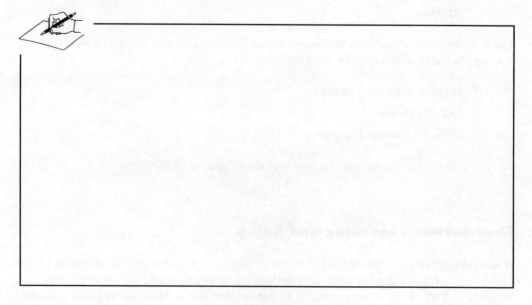

You need to introduce:

- variety
- activity
- a change of pace
- frequent breaks

into your training, to ensure that trainees remain fresh and alert.

Old and New Conflict

This is a shorthand way of saying that old and new behaviours can get in each other's way. At moments of stress it's easy to slide back into old routines from habit. So, as trainers, we need to make sure that new skills and behaviours are practised often enough to be well-grounded before trainees find themselves under stress. This explains why training in a crisis is not always effective.

Case Study

TJ Hocking, head warehouseman at BSN Furniture, had a team of three juniors, none of whom had much experience in picking and packing. When the company won a large order to supply furniture to a consortium of hospitals in the south of the country, there was a panic in the warehouse, and the three juniors muddled through, processing each batch for delivery manually. They had never had training in the computer system, because 'TJ' had looked after that side of things himself. Faced with a crisis, however, TJ sent his lads off for half a day's training each on the programme.

To his surprise — but not ours — the lads returned and proceeded to process the batches by hand. They needed the comfort of a familiar routine to see them through their time of stress. They promised to catch up with the training when they had time.

The lesson to be drawn from TJ Hocking's mistake is that training is not a fire-fighting tool. Rather, training implemented in good time and with due regard to probable future developments is a fire-preventer.

Inhibitions

We tend to forget or inhibit memories that are painful. Since change is often painful learning can also be blocked in this way. The implications of this for the training function are important.

There are many books written on the management of change, and to go into the details of it here would be inappropriate. In a nutshell, the key to success is to remove people's fear of change, and the only way to do that is to get them committed to the need for change and involved in the development of the nature of the change. All in all, it is a pretty tall order, and not one which the training function can undertake by itself.

In what circumstances might the training function be able successfully to build into its training provision features which would really get people committed to change? Write your answer in the box below.

· The training department can be successful in its efforts to
overcome fear and inhibitions if the whole organization is
committed to the changes, communicates the need for change, and
consults with the employees as often as possible.

Otherwise, the training department's efforts will seem thin and hollow. As
consultants, we have worked in organizations where the need for change has not
been communicated properly, as well as in more enlightened places. In the former,
if we ask employees about the need for change, the following responses are
common:

· 'No one's asked us that before!'

· 'It doesn't matter why we think it's happening, it's happening, and
that's that'

· 'Too late to worry about that now . . .'.

These people are prone to suppress and inhibit learning. In other organizations we
have heard different responses:

· 'We've got to keep our market edge'

· 'Other people change their product range really quickly — so can
we if we want to'.

These people are more likely to be motivated to learn and retain their new
knowledge.

Unless the training function has a voice at the highest level of decision making in
your organization, the problem of conscious or unconscious inhibition of learning is
likely to be a real one for you; from which you must conclude that it is crucial to
raise the profile of the training function so that you are listened to. This must be a
key element in your training strategy.

Summary

In this chapter you have seen that although learning is a natural process — so natural that you can't stop doing it — there are none the less factors at work in many situations which prevent the correct things from being learnt.

In one phrase, learning is hindered by **poor motivation**. People don't learn because, for one reason or another, consciously or unconsciously, they don't want to know. You examined these reasons in turn. They were:

- Unsuitable work environment — which involves relations between the learners, their bosses, their colleagues, and, of course, the job itself.

- Inappropriate subject matter — if it is irrelevant to people's jobs, they won't learn it.

- Past experience — learners may have picked up bad habits in their work which will tend to drown out new, better ideas received in training.

- Self-image — in situations where people's 'old jobs' have gone for good, learners feel particularly unvalued. Training which reinforces the worthlessness of the 'old skills' is going to be particularly hard to take.

- Inadequate study skills — learners unused to reading, writing and revising will find learning very hard if it involves these skills.

- Poor memory — 'poor' memory is caused by learners' inability to practise what they learn, to concentrate for long periods, and their instinct to suppress information which is painful to them.

Each of these 'blocks to learning' has implications for the training function which must take steps to ensure that they do not occur.

Assignment:

Go through five discrete elements in your training provision and write down for each one which 'blocks to learning' are likely to occur.

Then discuss with colleagues and line managers the steps you may take to eradicate these blocks.

Finally, devise a priority action plan so that everyone knows which blocks to learning are being addressed in which way.

Here is an example of the sort of document you will need to produce:

Training element	Block to learning	Steps to take
Machine operation	Bad habits from previous experience	Train line managers: • in correct methods • in supervising skills Discussed with: • T Ellis • J Ford • A Agnew

Actions:

1) Machine operations for supervisors 1st — 2nd March

2) Supervising skills for managers, workshops/open learning 8th — 12th March

3) Machine operation training for team 1 (supervisor to attend) 15th March

4) 'Probation period' team 1 operate under supervision 22nd — 25th March.

Enabling People to Learn

You are at the stage now where you have seen that although learning is a natural process, it doesn't always occur in the way you would like it to. Part of the skill of the trainer is to identify ways in which you can take advantage of the natural learning process, so that the things people learn will remain natural but will be relevant and important to people in the world of work.

By the time you've completed this chapter, you will be able to:

- list factors which encourage people to start learning
- list factors which encourage people to continue learning
- explain what it is about each factor which will allow you to enable learning to take place.

The Importance of Motivation

If there is one word which in itself would sum up this whole chapter, then that word is motivation. If you motivate people to learn, then they will learn — because people are naturally inclined to do what they are motivated to do, and disinclined to do what they are not motivated to.

On the other hand, if there is one word which is over-used without really being understood in this context, again, that word is motivation. Motivation to learn manifests itself in two forms which we will call **initial** and **continuous**. Consequently, this chapter will explore the factors which make people want to start learning, and then to continue learning.

Now we will pass the initiative over to you. (That's usually a good motivator!).

Rather than ask you what motivates you to learn — which is a fairly vague question — we'll phrase the question so that it has a sharper focus: what made you (a) buy this book (or take it from the shelf) and what made you (b) work through it this far?

Write your answers to those questions in this box.

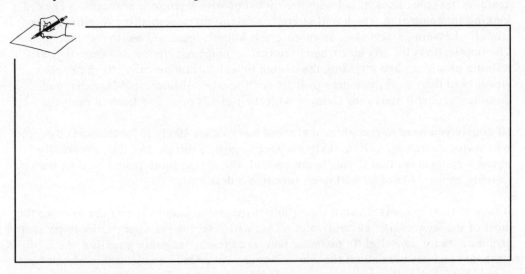

It would be really difficult to respond in detail to exactly what you've written there, but our experiences in various industrial situations over the years have led us to conclude that certain types of initial motivator and continuous motivator are very common. As you read through the next few pages you'll be able to judge for yourself just how typical — or otherwise — you are.

Initial Motivators

Initial Motivator 1: A New Challenge

Trainees are sometimes bored with their jobs, or with their normal routine. They're looking for something which will stretch or extend them, something to provide new stimuli. Learning a new skill or gaining new knowledge could well meet that need. The implications for you as a trainer are that by emphasizing the newness of your training provision, and stressing the degree to which training can refresh people's attitudes to their work, you may well attract a number of interested learners, and these learners will arrive for training with their minds open and keen to progress.

Of course you need to recognize that these learners are likely to be the sort of people who thrive on new stimuli, quickly get accustomed to things, and then eventually bored with them, so that if you're not careful, the escape route from boredom which training appeared to offer will itself turn into a dead end.

It is important to break down training into manageable chunks if you are to make the most of the 'new challenge' motivator. This will give you the opportunity to present each new chunk in a slightly different way and thereby maintain a feeling of freshness and newness about the whole course. An added benefit to this 'chunk-by-chunk' approach is that people gain in confidence with each completed element.

Case Study

Jennie Lucino was a researcher with Graxxon Enterprises. As part of her structured move into sales and marketing, she had to work through a series of cameos and case studies, each of which introduced her to a new type of client or a new situation. The trouble was that the formula for each cameo was always exactly the same, and Jennie's level of motivation began to fall. The trainer noted this and took the trouble to brief Jennie differently on each cameo unit, so that while the materials themselves stayed the same, she treated them differently. She was given different tasks — on one occasion she was asked to complete her own cameo document using the learning materials as a model to be improved upon. The result was that Jennie completed the training and moved into sales and marketing where she found that the milieu suited her temperament ideally.

Initial Motivator 2: The Wish to Succeed

Mention the wish to succeed and a certain personality type springs to mind: confident and dynamic, or, to be a little more negative, brash and thrusting. These people will be keen to learn provided they believe at the outset that training will ultimately give them what they need. Initially, they will be very keen, and this is a great opportunity for you to get off to a flying start. Because these people are self-motivated, some of the onus to motivate them is, initially at least, removed from the trainer.

But there are other types of individual — less sure of themselves but who none the less feel a desire to succeed. And success for these people may simply be the acquisition of a new skill or new knowledge. Feeling that taking part in training and learning more will make them worth more is enough to get them involved in training to start with. But it won't keep them there. Training design is very important for people like this who may be seriously discouraged by failure. Early success and rapid progress will give their confidence the boost it needs.

Initial Motivator 3: Personal Recommendation

This could be the one that applies to you in regard to this book; perhaps someone recommended it to you. It's often the case that people are motivated by others' recommendations in all aspects of training. People who take up training because of a recommendation usually present a very positive attitude. In many cases it is a friend who has recommended the training, and the friend will have stressed the way the trainee's temperament and personality will be suited to the materials. So far, so good.

As a trainer you will need to be aware that the 'friend' will not have assessed the trainee's experiences or abilities, and so there is a chance that the trainee's strong desire to learn is based on false or unrealistic expectations of what the course can do. A 'continuous' motivator will almost always be necessary if the trainee is to complete the course successfully.

Initial Motivator 4: A Way of Filling Time

It sounds rather negative and discouraging — that the training provision you so painstakingly prepare should be seen by many as just a way of filling in time. They have a slack month in the dispatch shed, and there they all are, clamouring for training.

What are (a) the dangers and (b) the opportunities which this situation presents to the trainer? Write your answers in this box.

The main danger is that you will interpret this desire for training negatively. Aware that the trainees wouldn't be there if they were busy, you think they're telling you that they don't rate training as a worthwhile activity. You become defensive and send out negative indicators, and this reinforces the trainees' perception of training as, well, less than enjoyable.

The opportunities, on the other hand, are there to be seized. You have a captive audience and, if you can provide interesting and stimulating training, then you could influence the trainees' attitude for the better. Next time, they could well see training as more than just a means of filling time.

In summary then, we can say that these initial motivators will start people off on training, but that you will need something more to encourage them to finish the course. We'll consider these 'continuous' motivators now.

Continuous Motivators

Continuous Motivator 1: Promotion

For some people, the successful outcome of training is promotion. And there are situations where certificated completion of a training course leads directly to professional advancement. The trainer in these situations will find learners are highly motivated to learn, complete the course, undertake examinations — everything. You should be aware that it is discouraging for people who seek promotion through training to face the prospect that even after training, the chances of promotion are very limited.

The challenge for the trainer in this situation is twofold. In the shorter term, you can help the learner to redefine success: 'You may not get promotion straight away, but you will be able to. . .' In the longer term — well, over to you:

What would you do in the longer term to improve the chances of your would-be promotion candidates being motivated to learn? Write your answer in this box.

In the longer term you could make it part of your strategy to ensure that the people responsible for promoting and advancing careers are aware of just how well your training fits people to meet greater responsibility within the organization.

You could also revise your training so that it genuinely addresses the criteria for promotion.

Continuous Motivator 2: Self-assurance

For some people, the success of a training course is equated with recognition and esteem. Trainees in this category need reassurance from their trainer and their peers that they are doing well. This places two responsibilities on your shoulders. First, there must be regular assessment as part of your courses, so that people who need to know how they are progressing can see and prove to themselves and others just what progress they are making. Second, throughout your courses and at regular intervals in your written materials you should include words and phrases like, 'That's good', 'Well done', and 'Congratulations'.

Continuous Motivator 3: Certification

The thought of getting some recognized accreditation for completing a piece of training is all the motivation some people need to stay motivated all the way through a course. Sometimes the thought of accreditation works as an initial motivator as well, but in our experience people can be deeply involved in a course before they realize that there is any accreditation at all; and then, when they do realize, the motivation levels rise.

At one end of the accreditation spectrum, there are nationally and even internationally recognized awards which people can work towards. At the other, there is the possibility of your creating your own in-house award system which could then be tied in to some form of incentive if you wished.

Continuous Motivator 4: Improved Performance

The greatest of all motivators is improved performance. Some people approach training in need of remedial help: they were failing in their job, and they knew it. For these people, the awareness that they are no longer failing, but succeeding, is a powerful motivator. Others approach training from a higher base: they're doing well, and they know it. Then, when they see they're doing even better, the sky's the limit.

For you as a trainer, the task is to ensure that training is:

- relevant
- up-to-date
- well matched to the needs of the job.

Continuous Motivator 5: Training Design

The training itself can help to motivate, but it cannot motivate in the face of de-motivating factors on all other fronts. Assuming, however, that people are initially motivated, and then continuously motivated by the thought of success, training design can help.

- The training should be designed so that the motivators discussed above stand out.
- Courses and materials should be presented to a professional standard.
- Learning materials and courses should be objectives-driven, with regular assessment of learner progress and evaluation of the material's effectiveness.

To sum up the continuous motivators above, the key every time is **success**. People want to succeed, but they differ as to what they understand by the word success. The training materials themselves should appear 'successful' — that is to say not shoddy, scrappy or makeshift. And most importantly of all, the learner should be able to make the logical link between the training they are doing and the success they need.

It would be wrong to leave out a 'motivator' which often persuades people to attend training courses, to work through written materials, and to persist even when the going gets tough. We deliberately haven't included it in our list of initial or continuous motivators, because in our opinion it is troublesome, and causes resentment.

The questions to you are: (a) what is this powerful but very suspect motivator? and (b) how can you gain some advantage from the situation?

Before you write your answers in the box, we'll give one more clue: this motivator is perhaps the most often heard response when we ask why people are doing our courses. Write your answers now.

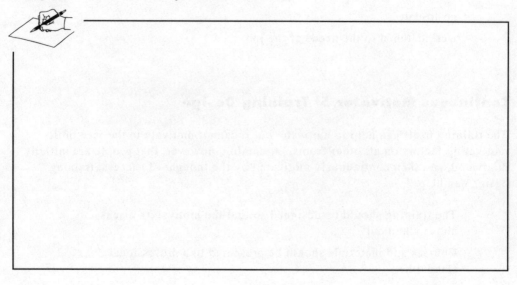

The motivator is 'The boss sent me'.

And as for turning it to your advantage, well, remember the basic theory of learning.

Part of your strategy must be to propagate the theory of learning which states that there is no teaching as such, only the ability to allow and encourage learning to take place. It follows from this that you should target your line managers and explain to them why it is important to **allow their people to learn** rather than 'get their people trained'.

Case Study

Alan Dobbs was for years in charge of training at UBB Plastics, and one of his best customers was Isobel Hoskins from Support Services who insisted that all her team go through his three-stage staff development programme. Trainees from Support Services were always there in number, but were often remarkable for their lack of enthusiasm. '**She** sent us', was all they would say — in the kindest possible way, of course, but even so, no one from Support Services ever actually chose to be trained.

Alan approached Isobel and asked her to try a different tack; to leave it up to the people when they wanted to come, and to take some responsibility for their own development. Isobel agreed to encourage rather than to coerce.

In brief, the numbers fell — initially — but those from Support Services who did attend got far more out of it and were noticeably more effective members of the team when they returned to their tasks. This led to an increased take-up of training on a voluntary basis from Support Services staff, and increased impact on the performance of the Support team.

Isobel was pleased (though some say reluctant) to comment on the increase in initiative and responsibility in her team.

Summary

In the course of this chapter you saw first of all how motivation is the key to enabling people to learn.

This was followed by an examination of four initial motivators — factors which persuade people to subscribe to learning in the first place.

Next there came five continuous motivators — factors which keep people motivated to learn right through to the end.

As a final point you looked at a common 'motivator' — 'The boss sent me'. You saw that this was not really a motivator at all, and that it is in fact more likely to cause resentment than anything else. The ultimate solution to this problem is to change the attitude of the bosses in question so that they encourage people to learn rather than ordering them.

Assignment:
As part of the introduction to one or more of your elements of training, get trainees to tell you (or write down for you):

- *why they came on the training*
- *what they expect to get out of it*
- *what they would ideally expect to get out of it (if different!).*

Compile the results and then call a meeting at which:

- *yourself*
- *your team*
- *representatives of the trainees*
- *appropriate managers*

are invited to brainstorm ways in which training can capitalize on those things which motivate learners and avoid things which demotivate them.

Draw up an action plan.

Learning Styles

If you've reached this stage in the book, you will be aware that there is no such thing as the 'standard learner'. We're all learners because we're all learning all the time, and it's self-evident that we're all different.

The previous chapter in particular raised issues about people who are confident to the point of being brash, and those who are under-confident to the point of needing constant reassurance. How is the trainer best to come to terms with the sheer variety of learners in every organization? Where do you start?

By the time you've completed this chapter, you will be able to:

- describe the four stages in the learning cycle
- describe the four types of learner as identified by Mumford and Honey
- suggest practical ways in which you can help all your learners improve their learning skills
- suggest ways in which your learning provision can be improved so as to accommodate each type of learner.

The Learning Cycle

Given that we're all learning all the time, it would be facile to maintain that learning is a linear process: some form of study followed by some form of practice and that's that. The fact of the matter is that learning is a cyclical process, or, to be even more accurate, an upwardly spiralling process which goes on and on, repeating the same stages again and again from a base of ever increasing skills and knowledge.

This situation would be potentially difficult for the trainer to come to terms with, were it not for the pioneering work done by David Kolb who identified the four stages in the learning cycle, and also went on to build them into a working model which has been an invaluable aid to trainers ever since.

We've reproduced the model in the diagram below, and to help you get involved in it as soon as possible, we've provided just the title of each stage in the cycle. We'd like you to write in the box under each one what sort of learning, or what sort of thought-processes are happening at that point in the cycle.

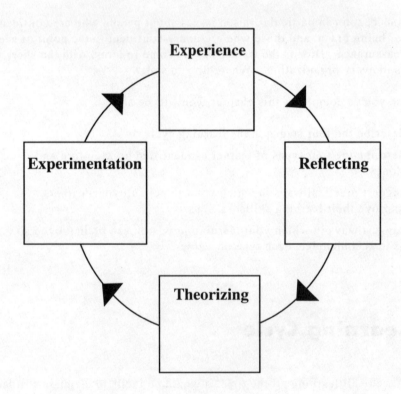

We'll start at the top and have a look at each one in some detail.

Experience

The most common form of learning by experience takes place away from the training environment altogether, that is to say, at the workplace.

Consider again your experience of driving a car, if that's appropriate for you. When you had passed your driving test, you could not claim that you'd learnt all there was to learn about driving. Even after months or years of experience, that is still a bold claim to make! But our point is made. Learning by experience is a major part of the natural learning process.

The question then arises of the significance of this fact for the trainer. An extreme (and in our view erroneous) answer would be that the trainer's responsibility ends when actual work begins. This idea, if taken to its logical conclusion, divorces training from the world of work and is ultimately detrimental to individuals and organizations alike, so we will pursue it no further.

Instead you should focus on the more fruitful path of seeing the ways in which training can benefit from the fact that much of our learning comes from experience, and the ways in which training can enhance the quality of that learning. There is, in short, a major opportunity for another upward spiral — this time in the relationship between training and learning.

When the learner is in the workplace, the trainer has an opportunity to evaluate the training which has been provided and the learning which has occurred. This will give feedback which will enable the trainer to adapt and develop training provision within the organization so that learning can be improved in the future.

When the learner is in training — away from the workplace — what do you think the trainer can do to ensure that learning from experience occurs? Write at least two practical suggestions in this box.

The suggestions we came up with were:

- simulating practical work
- playing games
- group discussions
- practising new skills in a safe environment.

There is a high degree of overlap between the ideas above, and which you choose will depend on the situation you are in and the job you're training for. Pilots learn in flight simulators to acquire experience in a safe environment. Soldiers and tacticians play war-games to experience dangers without actually getting shot at, and counsellors take part in discussions so they can share in other people's experiences and learn.

The diagram on the next page illustrates the upward spiral effects of learning through experience. Notice how practice reinforces the learning by experience and builds into confidence, and out of confidence comes a need for more advanced learning.

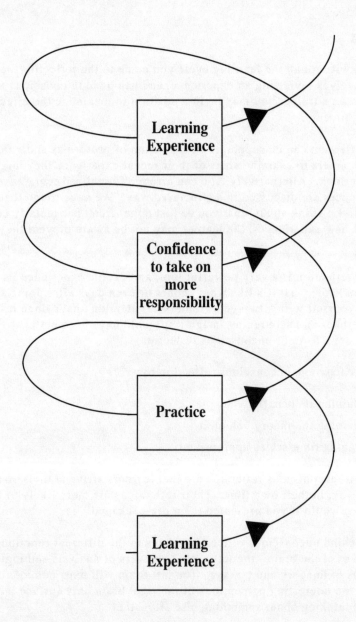

Reflecting

Moving clockwise round the learning cycle you come to the reflecting stage. Reflecting involves reviewing an experience, and can be both conscious and unconscious. As a trainer you may be in a position to maximize the effectiveness of the reflecting process.

Conscious reflection can be supported by provision of proformas and guidelines which force learners to examine areas of their recent experience they might otherwise overlook. Alternatively, you can arrange formalized review sessions where experiences are discussed in a structured way. We have found that bland instructions like, 'Think about what you've just done' aren't particularly effective, as, in the case of new experiences, the learner may not be aware of what they've just done.

Unconscious reflection is a very powerful tool, and people experience its effects all the time. You know what it's like when, hours or even days after doing something, you surprise yourself with a twinge of remorse: 'I shouldn't have done it like that. . .' or perhaps an encouraging insight: 'It would have been better if I'd . . .' Dreams, too, are a form of unconscious reflection.

Trainers can encourage unconscious reflection by:

- explaining its benefits
- explaining the theory behind it
- arranging time-scales appropriately.

The benefits of unconscious reflection are that learners arrive at their own insights, in their own way, in their own time. Their reflections are more likely to remain with them than they would if you presented them pre-packaged.

The theory behind unconscious reflection relates to the different functions of different halves of the brain: the left with its powers of analysis and logic, the right with strengths of imagery and fantasy. The left brain will most commonly be used at work, and the interesting perceptions of the right brain only surface later, when the learner is thinking about something else altogether.

Following from this theory, trainers can alert learners to the benefits of relaxation and changes of activity as part of the learning process. You can also stress the importance of thinking in images and pictures.

Timescales for feedback should allow learners to relax and consider over a period of time just what they've learnt.

Theorizing

The third stage of the learning cycle as analysed here is theorizing. Theorizing involves:

- conceptualizing
- relating ideas to experience and models
- interpreting something.

Conceptualizing

There is a stage in learning when everything has to be turned into ideas, so that the mind can work through what is going on. This is the only way that improvements can be made, the only way changes can be suggested, and at an even more basic level, it's the only way people can ever talk about what it is they're supposed to be learning.

The trainer can help the conceptualizing part of the process by providing the learners with what they need. This could be:

- time — to think things through, talk them over and prepare ideas
- resources — access to information, awareness of sources of relevant facts
- vocabulary — to enable people to discuss their ideas, and also as an aid to memory
- opportunities — to meet and compare ideas.

We must add a word of caution about conceptualizing, namely:

- conceptualizing is a means to an end, not an end in itself.

There are people who are naturally inclined to conceptualize, and build their inclination into a talent. If not checked this can lead to their being able to theorize and discuss articulately and informatively, but without much relation to reality.

Vocabulary is a case in point. Used as a tool to enable discussion, a certain amount of jargon is useful. Taken to excess, jargon becomes the domain of the few used to exclude others and make them feel inferior, and it becomes divorced from people's needs.

In brief, make sure the ideas are your servant — and not the other way round.

Relating ideas to experience and models

An important second step in theorizing is comparing and contrasting ideas either to experience (as is the case when theorizing follows practice) or to a model (as is the case when theorizing precedes practice).

This is essentially an intellectual activity, and the trainer can ensure its success by:

- arranging access to the models — making sure that when the trainees come up with their ideas, there is some focus for their discussion.

Case Study

Part of Alan Dobbs' stage two development training at UBB Plastics was a series on elementary decision making. After an introductory session, trainees were given, where possible, tasks to perform at the workplace which involved decision making. As part of the follow-up, Alan ran a course where he presented alternative criteria for decision making — criteria which are well-known and respected, but unfamiliar to the learners under Alan's tutelage. The result was always a high level of discussion and debate in the training sessions. The trainees themselves always commented that having confronted other models of decision making, they were better able to explain and defend the decisions they actually made.

Interpreting

Interpreting gives the learner the opportunity to find out what models, theories and ideas actually mean in their own situation. Thus a course on supervisory skills might contain a clear exposition of what people need to do, but inside the learner's head there is interpretation taking place: 'How does that fit in with what I know about John? and Michelle . . ?'

Interpreting also enables the learner to take their experiences and build them into theories, so that they can use what they know to create strategies for themselves in the future.

Experimentation

In a phrase, experimentation involves trying things out in a practical way — but it's different from learning by experience.

What do you think is the main difference between learning by experience and learning by experimentation? Put your answer in this box.

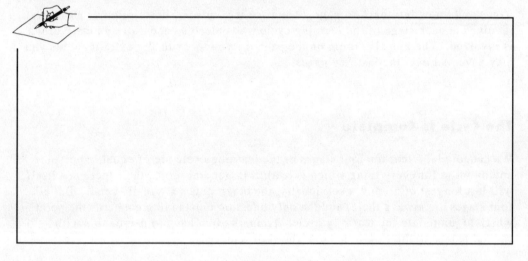

Learning by experience has its emphasis on doing — and the learning happens as an important but secondary function of the task being performed.

Learning by experimentation is very practical and may be task-based, but the emphasis is on the learning. The whole thrust is towards exploring, finding out, discovering, and more often than not there is no purpose other than learning to the task being performed.

There are other differences as well. You can, for example, learn from other people's experiences, but you cannot learn from their experimentation. In experimentation, there is a close relationship between the learner and the novelty of what they are going through.

You should now turn back to page 70 and see if your brief description of what was involved at each stage of the learning cycle was indeed an accurate summary of what is involved. There is also room on the page for you to write any extra thoughts you may have had over the last few pages.

The Cycle is Complete

We cannot claim that the four stages of the learning cycle are of equal importance and duration for every thing which is learnt. In general terms, the experience itself will last longest of all and, occasionally, the other stages are really small. But all four stages are always there, and the only question outstanding concerns the point at which to jump onto the learning cycle. Trainers often have to decide this with special regard to the task in hand or the skill required.

Case Study

A large government body decided to introduce a new computer system which would allow it to process all its business much more quickly. The trainers realized that allowing the learners to start at the experience phase and move on through reflection to the others was to court disaster, because the amount of errors caused immediately following introduction would be enormous. Instead, they plumped for a session of theory, where learners were shown what to expect, followed by experimentation, where each learner was allowed to 'play around' with a mock-up of the system before it went live. They organized a feedback session three weeks after the launch of the new system so that learners could reflect not only on their learning experience, but also on the teething troubles they had been experiencing.

We would like to report that the launch went without a hitch, but of course it didn't. Predictably, there were glitches of all sorts, but the general perception was of a remarkably smooth change-over, considering the size of the operation.

Case Study

A large teacher training college in eastern Scotland insists that all their would-be teachers spend a month in a school alongside the teaching staff to gain experience before they begin their formal studies. They reason (and this is completely in keeping with the learning cycle) that experience followed by a period of reflection is the ideal base on which to build theories which can be applied — first in a controlled environment, such as in front of a selected class under strict supervision, and later in an actual teaching situation. The learning cycle is complete, though it has started from a different point.

You will hear many home-spun theories in connection with the learning cycle:

'All our people are thoroughly trained before they're allowed to deal with the public . . . '

'I believe people are best when they're thrown in at the deep end . . .'

The point is, in many cases, that people who have learnt in one way feel that everyone else ought to learn in the same way; and that may or may not be the case. We believe that the skill of the trainer lies in determining at which point the training for a certain task ought to begin.

As we intimated above, the job itself may give a good clue as to which would be the best point to start the cycle. But there is another important factor to be taken into consideration. Look at this rather old case study . . .

Case Study

Beethoven was a pupil of both Haydn and Mozart, and went to them to learn, amongst other things, counterpoint. Both his teachers told how Beethoven learnt nothing from them. The only way he ever learnt anything, they complained, was by going away and making mistakes.

The question we put to you is this: What 'type' of learner was Beethoven? Or, to put it another way, at what point in the learning cycle do you think he preferred to start?

Write your answers in here.

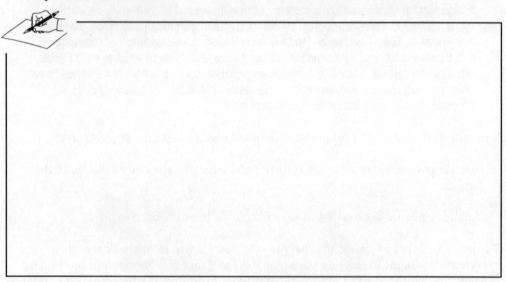

Beethoven was an activist. If you've chosen a different word or phrase to describe that 'have-a-go' mentality, then fine. These people like to start the learning cycle at the experience stage; not for them boring old theory!

This serves only as an example. Peter Honey and Alan Mumford have identified **four different** 'types' of learner, and I have drawn from their work over the past few years in preparing the remaining pages of this chapter which deals with different people's preferred learning styles.

Types of Learner

The diagram below shows the types of learner described in one word only. We've left space under each for you to describe the sort of character you might expect each to have.

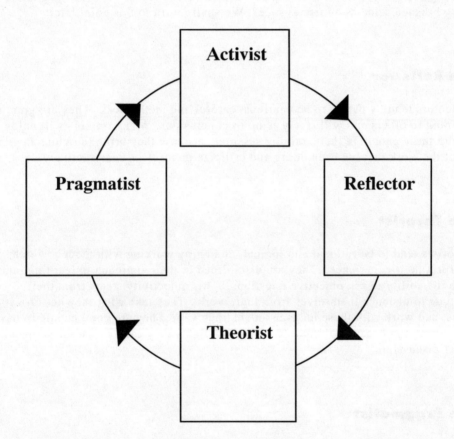

The Activist

Activists are, as in the case of Beethoven, keen to have a go. You can expect them to be impetuous, impatient, untroubled at the thought of getting something wrong, open-minded and flexible. These are people who will not baulk at being asked to do something new or outside their normal routine. As a trainer, you might find yourself wincing at the prospect at enabling people like this to learn. How can you avoid being brushed aside as an irrelevance? We shall return to this point later.

The Reflector

Reflectors tend by nature to be cautious, careful and methodical. They are good at listening to others and will rarely jump to conclusions. Many trainers will enjoy having these people in their training sessions, because they bring judicious insights about the work they've been doing and criticize themselves constructively.

The Theorist

Theorists tend to be rational and logical, and enjoy working with models which interpret their experience. They are disciplined in their approach to learning, and have the ability to ask objective questions. This objectivity stems from their aptitude to distance themselves from their work. They take what they do, turn it into ideas, and work with these ideas in an abstract way. They are good people to have in a discussion because of the interesting sidelights they can cast on the subject under discussion.

The Pragmatist

Pragmatists are planners; they are practical and down to earth. They enjoy nothing more than actually trying things out and making them work. They seek early opportunities to experiment with applications, and if you have them on a course, they'll be keen for it to finish so they can get back to the workplace and try one or two things out.

What This Means For You

You'll notice that we mentioned after each of the learner types above, something about their relationship to trainers and the training provision. The existence of these four types of learner is something that you will have to cope with if you are to do your job well.

The point is that to be most effective, your training provision must do two things:

- first, taking a reactive stance, it must accommodate all four learning types

- second, in a proactive mode, it should develop the learners themselves so that any one individual is at least capable of getting something worthwhile out of all four stages in the learning cycle.

Reactivity

The first thing to do is to analyse just what each learner type is seeking from training, and to help you to do that, we've created the following grid. True, most of it is blank at the moment, but that's only because we want to involve you in the process as much as possible.

The first column shows the type of learner. The second shows roughly what they want from training. The third — which you will fill in — describes the sort of training which could give them what they need. The fourth is for you to write in which elements of your current training provision fall into that category.

Fill in the boxes now.

Learner	Wants	Type of Training	My Provision
Activists:	Experience Variety Excitement Activity People		
Reflectors:	Objective data to draw conclusions Chance to reflect Chance to analyse Chance to deliberate		
Theorists	Models Theorems Complexity Perfection Rationality Coherence		
Pragmatists	Chance to experiment New ideas New theories New techniques Practical applications Solutions to problems		

Here are our thoughts on the matter. We've left the fourth column blank again, because we can't say what your current provision is. We do, however, make some comment at the end.

Learner	Wants	Type of Training	My Provision
Activists:	Experience Variety Excitement Activity People	Group-based Experiential Learning by doing Group reviews Lively debate	
Reflectors:	Objective data to draw conclusions Chance to reflect Chance to analyse Chance to deliberate	Distance learning Private study Audio Video	
Theorists	Models Theorems Complexity Perfection Rationality Coherence	Computer-based Training Electronic Inter- activity Models Simulators	
Pragmatists	Chance to experiment New ideas New theories New techniques Practical applications Solutions to problems	Controlled experience Personal coaching On-the-job training	

If you find that your current provision contains elements to meet all these needs, then you're well on the way to reacting appropriately to the different types of learner. Should you find that, say, your activists are inadequately catered for, then you should set up some appropriate training for them without delay.

Proactivity

In the ideal world, all learners would benefit from all stages in the learning cycle equally. Unfortunately, they don't. And it causes problems for individuals, trainers and organizations alike. You may well have worked alongside people who rush at problems and learn from the mistakes they make; the learning can be a long process and it can turn out to be expensive, too, depending on the size of the mistakes. Similarly you may have worked with people who know the theory of how things are done, but, when they come to putting it into practice, they struggle. The trainer has to take each of these people and get them involved with all four stages of the learning process: but how?

The first step is to ensure that whatever is to be learnt can be addressed from all four points in the cycle. There is no purpose in telling activists that they ought to study a little theory if there is no theory available.

The second step is to **sell the benefits**.

Our experience is that the best way of restraining activists is to demonstrate that a little theorizing before (or after, depending on the task) will make their activity more effective, because effectiveness is a major motivator for people who want to do things and establish a reputation as achievers.

Theorists can get 'hooked' on training, as the notion of learning for its own sake is attractive to them. What's more, being this learning type, their own educational experience may have involved a lot of pure, unapplied learning. One way of addressing these people is to provide logical, reasoned arguments as to why practical training is so important and an explanation of what benefits it will bring to them.

Similarly, reflectors can be given data to analyse and pore over, and the data will prove that theorizing, experimentation and experience are all important parts of the learning experience. Pragmatists can be encouraged to experiment — once completely unprepared, and then another time after some practical experience and an opportunity to reflect.

We recommend that all your training should consider, as part of its stated aims and objectives, where it fits into the learning cycle. Thus one of the stated aims of a hands-on computer course would be:

· 	to apply the theories learnt in. . . .

which makes it clear that the hands-on element is only part of a package. If there is to be a follow-up course, then this too should be made clear at the outset.

Identifying Learner Types

A lot of the skill in identifying learner types comes with experience. Just talk to some people and you'll know within a minute the type of learner they are.

Honey and Mumford have developed a questionnaire which will enable you to assemble more formal information on the learner types. With their kind permission, we have reproduced an abridged version of it as the Appendix to this book. The assignment at the end of the Chapter requires you to use this questionnaire in your organization.

Summary

In this final chapter, you have looked at:

- the four stages of the learning cycle, which were:
  — experience
  — reflecting
  — theorizing
  — experimentation.

You saw that:

- this cycle is more accurately described as an upward spiral
- there is no right or wrong place to start the cycle; rather, it all depends on the job or the skill being acquired and on the 'learning type' of the individual.

You went on to see that:

- there are four identifiable types of learner
  — activists
  — reflectors
  — theorists
  — pragmatists
- each one prefers a different stage of the learning cycle
- you can **react** to this situation by making sure that learners get the type of training most suited to them
- you can **proact** by working on the individuals, and enabling them to get the best out of other stages in the learning cycle, particularly those which do not naturally match their temperament
- all-round learners are the best learners.

Assignment:

Take one item of your training provision and describe it according to the table on page 83 of this book. For example, if your induction training is group-based, but has an element of private study to it, then make a note to that effect.

Get the trainees who are involved in that item of training to complete the abridged version of Honey and Mumford's Learning Styles Questionnaire in the Appendix to this book. Instructions for using and interpreting the questionnaire are likewise in the Appendix.

Do their references match the training you're providing? A group with strong activist and reflector tendencies would appreciate the mix of group based work and private study.

Or — is there a mis-match?

If so, make a list of the actions you will take to improve your training provision.

Alternatively, you may find certain individuals who have a low preference for an important learning style. Write down how you can persuade these people to become more involved in a learning style which at present doesn't motivate them much.

You should note that the figures used in this assignment are based on norms taken from all walks of life. For a more detailed and accurate picture focused more sharply on the questionnaire results you could expect in a specific business or occupation, you should obtain a copy of Honey and Mumford's Manual of Learning Styles (P. Honey) (1992 Edition).

Appendix

Honey and Mumford's Manual of Learning Styles an Abridged Questionnaire

Instructions

The questionnaire can be used to analyse your own learning type or, if you choose to distribute it to a group of your people, to give you a picture of what their learning styles are.

The instructions for administering the questionnaire are very simple. Just turn the page and start, and when you're finished, turn the page again to see how to interpret your results. (If you're distributing the questionnaire, respondents should be given the two question pages to fill in, and then it's up to you whether you collect them in and interpret the results or distribute the interpretation page as well. The latter course of action is recommended.)

I stress again that this abridged version of the questionnaire will not necessarily give as accurate a picture as would the full questionnaire which you will find in Honey and Mumford's *Manual of Learning Styles*.

The Questionnaire

This questionnaire is designed to find out your preferred learning style(s). Over the years you have probably developed learning 'habits' which help you benefit more from some experiences than from others.

Since you are probably unaware of this, this questionnaire will help you pinpoint your learning preferences, so that you are in a better position to select learning experiences that suit your style.

There is no time-limit to this questionnaire. It will probably take you 10-15 minutes. The accuracy of the results depend on how honest you can be. There are no right or wrong answers.

If you agree more than you disagree with a statement, put a tick by it. If you disagree more than you agree, put a cross. Be sure to mark each item with either a tick or a cross.

☐ 1. I often take reasonable risks if I feel it justified.

☐ 2. I tend to solve problems using a step-by-step approach, avoiding any fanciful ideas.

☐ 3. I have a reputation for having a no-nonsense direct style.

☐ 4. I often find that actions based on feelings are as sound as those based on careful thought and analysis.

☐ 5. The key factor in judging a proposed idea or solution is whether it works in practice or not.

☐ 6. When I hear about a new idea or approach I like to start working out how to apply it in practice as soon as possible.

☐ 7. I like to follow a self-disciplined approach, establish clear routines and logical thinking patterns.

☐ 8. I take pride in doing a thorough, methodical job.

☐ 9. I get on best with logical, analytical people, and less well with spontaneous, 'irrational' people.

☐ 10. I take care over the interpretation of data available to me, and avoid jumping to conclusions.

☐ 11. I like to reach a decision carefully after weighing up many alternatives.

☐ 12. I'm attracted more to new, unusual ideas than practical ones.

☐ 13. I dislike situations that I cannot fit into a coherent pattern.

☐ 14. I like to relate my action to a general principle.

☐ 15. In meetings I have a reputation of going straight to the point, no matter what others feel.

☐ 16. I prefer to have as many sources of information as possible — the more data to consider the better.

☐ 17. Flippant people who don't take things seriously enough usually irritate me.

☐ 18. I prefer to respond to events on a spontaneous flexible basis rather than plan things out in advance.

☐ 19. I dislike very much having to present my conclusions under the time pressure of tight deadlines, when I could have spent more time thinking about the problem.

☐ 20. I usually judge other people's ideas principally on their practical merits.

☐ 21. I often get irritated by people who want to rush headlong into things.

☐ 22. The present is much more important than thinking about the past or future.

☐ 23. I think that decisions based on a thorough analysis of all the information are sounder than those based on intuition.

☐ 24. In meetings I enjoy contributing ideas to the group, just as they occur to me.

☐ 25. On balance I tend to talk more than I should, and ought to develop my listening skills.

☐ 26. In meetings I get very impatient with people who lose sight of the objectives.

☐ 27. I enjoy communicating my ideas and opinions to others.

☐ 28. People in meetings should be realistic, keep to the point, and avoid indulging in fancy ideas and speculations.

☐ 29. I like to ponder many alternatives before making up my mind.

☐ 30. Considering the way my colleagues react in meetings, I reckon on the whole I am more objective and unemotional.

☐ 31. At meetings I'm more likely to keep in the background, than to take the lead and do most of the talking.

☐ 32. On balance I prefer to do the listening than the talking.

☐ 33. Most times I believe the end justifies the means.

☐ 34. Reaching the group's objectives and targets should take precedence over individual feelings and objectives.

☐ 35. I do whatever seems necessary to get the job done.

☐ 36. I quickly get bored with methodical, detailed work.

☐ 37. I am keen on exploring the basic assumptions, principles and theories underpinning things and events.

☐ 38. I like meetings to be run on methodical lines sticking to laid-down agenda.

☐ 39. I steer clear of subjective or ambiguous topics.

☐ 40. I enjoy the drama and excitement of a crisis.

Now turn over and see how to interpret the answers.

How to Interpret your Answers

The numbers of the questions you've just ticked or crossed appear distributed in the columns below. Score 2 marks for each question you ticked, and 0 for all those you crossed. Then total each column.

1		8		2		3	
4		10		7		5	
12		11		9		6	
18		16		13		15	
22		19		14		20	
24		21		17		26	
25		23		30		28	
27		29		37		33	
36		31		38		34	
40		32		39		35	
Activist Total		Reflector Total		Theorist Total		Pragmatist Total	

Now ring your totals as they appear in the chart below. Where do your preferences lie? What sort of learner are you?

Activist	Reflector	Theorist	Pragmatist	
20	20	20	20	
19				
18		19		
17			19	Very strong preference
16	19	18		
15			18	
14		17		
13	18	16	17	
12	17	15	16	
	16			Strong preference
11	15	14	15	
10	14	13	14	
9	13	12	13	Moderate preference
8				
7	12	11	12	
6	11	10	11	
5	10	9	10	Low preference
4	9	8	9	
3	8	7	8	
	7	6	7	
	6	5	6	
2	5	4	5	
	4		4	Very low preference
1	3	3	3	
	2	2	2	
	1	1	1	
0	0	0	0